Short*ish* wa in north Cornwall

Paul White

Bossiney Books · Launceston

This reprint 2007
First published 2004 by
Bossiney Books Ltd, Langore, Launceston, Cornwall PL15 8LD
www.bossineybooks.co.uk
Copyright © 2004 Paul White
All rights reserved
ISBN 978-189938366-5

Acknowledgements
The maps are by Graham Hallowell
Cover design by Heards Design Partnership
Photographs by the author
Printed in Great Britain by R Booth Ltd, Mabe, Cornwall

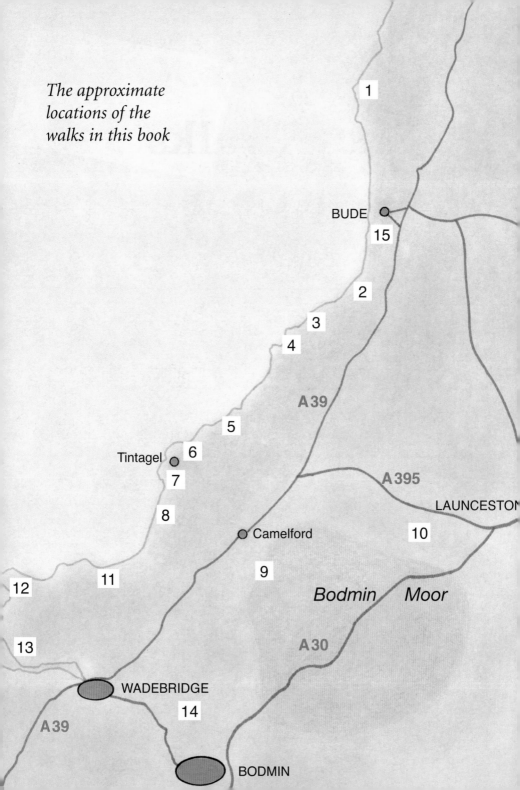

The approximate locations of the walks in this book

Introduction

For ease of understanding we have defined 'north Cornwall' in this book as the area east of the Camel estuary and north of the A30. (North Cornwall District Council's territory extends beyond this, and includes Padstow.) A companion volume, *Shortish Walks St Ives to Padstow*, was published in 2006. We have largely omitted walks on Bodmin Moor, which we hope to cover in a future book.

A 'shortish' walk is intended to take a couple of hours or so, and is typically 6-8 km (4-5 miles) in length. How long you actually take will depend on your fitness, enthusiasm, and the weather conditions. All the walks are circular, and the majority involve a section of the cliff path with a rural return. There are three wholly inland walks.

Safety

Cliff walking can be very exposed; the wind-chill factor is like being out in the Atlantic, and of course Cornish weather can change very rapidly, so you need to carry extra layers of clothing, as well as water-proofs, for what is often an abrupt change of temperature between inland and cliff walking.

Many of the walks involve fairly strenuous ascents and descents, especially on the coast path. Proper walking boots are vital for grip and ankle support, and a walking pole or stick is useful for balance in the descents. On the inland sections in particular you may well find muddy patches even in dry weather, not to mention briars, thistles and nettles, all of which thrive in our soil, so bare legs are a liability.

The main hazard of walking the cliff path is that for most of the way it is not fenced off from the drop. Go no nearer the edge than you have to: you might be standing on an overhang. Take great care when the path does take you near the edge, and keep a close eye on children and dogs. In many places the cliffs are eroding, so respect diversions.

The maps provided in this book look very attractive but they are only intended as sketch maps, so you may well want to carry an OS 1:25,000 map. OS grid references are given where needed.

The Cornish countryside

Despite many pressures on their livelihoods, Cornish farmers are still trying to make a living from the land you pass through. Please respect their crops; if a few of them haven't yet restored the route of the foot-path through their fields, no doubt they'll do so 'd'rec'ly', so go round the edge of the field! Leave gates closed or open as you find them, and keep dogs under control, especially during the lambing season.

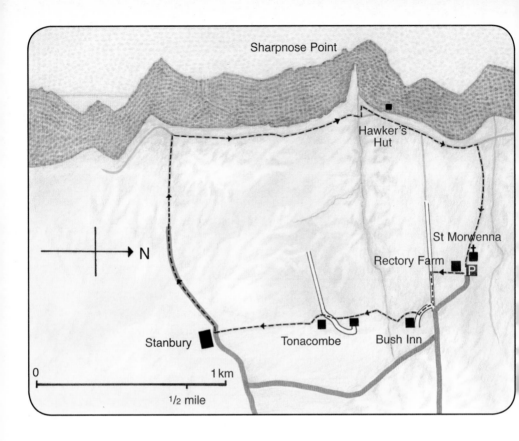

Walk 1 Morwenstow

Distance: 5.8 km (3 1/2 miles) Time: 2 hours OS Explorer sheet 126
Character: A pleasant inland section, then stunning coastline, famous
as the home of Parson Robert Hawker – minor Victorian poet, first-rate
eccentric, and rescuer of shipwrecked corpses. One very steep descent
and ascent on coast path; vertiginous in places.

Park at Morwenstow Church (SS 206153), where Rectory Farm offers
excellent refreshments in season. Walk up past the front of the farm,
through a waymarked gate, over a stile and across a field to a gated
stile. Turn left along the track. Bear right when you come to the green
and take the footpath through the small double gate across the back
of the Bush Inn. Bear left to the bottom of a small field (which dou-
bles as the pub garden). Cross two stiles, then down a field to a third.
Descend the steps then turn left to a stile and across a stream. Up what
looks like an ancient packhorse track.

    Proceed in a more or less straight line over five stiles, to a woodland
path. After another stile, cross a farm track and take the stile ahead,

passing Tonacombe, a Tudor manor house with a rather grand gateway. Up the field edge on the left and follow round until you reach a stile at the top (watch out for a tricky sloping stone as you descend from the stile). Then across the field ahead: you will see the strange shapes of the Government 'radio station' emerging above the crop. Cross a stile into a lane, and turn right. (The farm is Stanbury, and is again Tudor and in part earlier.)

Pass two useful car parks, not shown on the OS map, and keep straight on, signed TO THE COASTPATH. After a number of stiles, turn right along the coast path.

Pass the dramatic promontory called Sharpnose Point. After entering National Trust land at Tidna Shute, turn left back towards the sea (or keep right uphill for a shortcut) and walk out on a spectacular narrow headland. There is a waterfall marked on the map but it's out of sight. Return the same way, then bear left, very steeply for 200 m, gaining 80 m in altitude in that distance!

Ignore a path on the right and continue through a kissing-gate. On the left is Hawker's Hut, where the vicar contemplated the ocean and smoked opium. Back to the main path, and continue until you can see the church tower on your right. Cross a field back to your car.

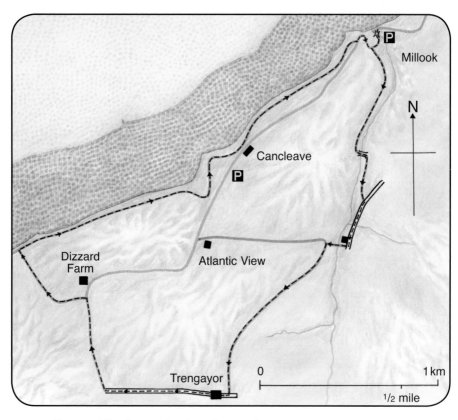

Walk 2 Millook, south of Widemouth Bay

Distance: 8.3 km (5 1/4 miles) Time: 2 1/4 hours OS Explorer sheet 111
Character: A very fine walk – perhaps the only one in this book where
the coastal section can (in the right conditions) be bettered by the
inland section: magical woodland.

There can occasionally be a problem with parking for this walk.
Ideally, park at the foot of the valley at Millook (SX 185000) where
there is space for several cars. Failing that, park at Cancleave, 1 km
south of Millook on the coast road, where there is space for 4 cars, and
start by going north up the coast path. And if that also is full, there's
a largish car park just north of Millook, but that adds a substantial
ascent and descent to the walk.

   From Millook, ascend the lane southwards to the first corner, where
a PUBLIC FOOTPATH leads inland. Go through 2 gates and along a track.
At a ford, cross the footbridge and turn right through woodland. A
stile leads to a path through a meadow full of wildflowers in Spring
and Summer. Leave the meadow by a stile at the far left side and take

6

The beach at Millook has some amazing geology, and is well worth a visit

When did you last see a woodland scene like this?

the track towards DIZZARD & TRENGAYOR. Pass the back of a house and turn right through a kissing gate; cross a stile and footbridge, climb a few steps and turn left.

After winding through more beautiful woodland the path ascends a holloway – an ancient road, sometimes muddy as they tend to be. At the top of the holloway go through a gate and turn right along a track, past a farm (gates) and out to a lane.

Turn right and after 450 m turn left TO THE COASTPATH. Pass through two gates and keep left down a track. From a stile a way-marked path leads down the right side of two fields to a (somewhat hidden) footbridge. Cross and turn right uphill through a wood then across cliff pasture, taking a line where you climb gently to a small gate where you turn right onto the coast path, on which (hopefully!) you can't get lost on your way back to Millook.

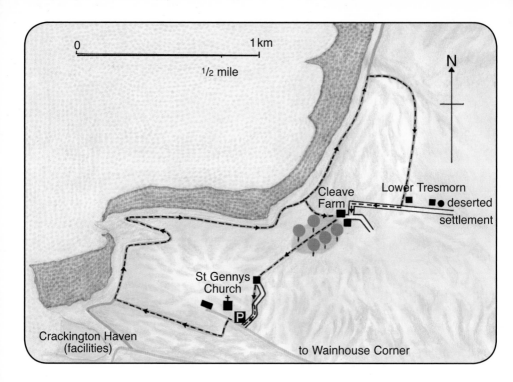

Walk 3   St Gennys

Distance for the full circuit: 6km (3³/4 miles) Time: 2 hours
Distance for the short walk: 3.6km (2¹/4 miles), 1¹/4 hours
OS Explorer sheet 111
Character: Dramatic cliff scenery, with a steep descent and ascent even
on the short walk, and two on the longer walk.

St Gennys Churchtown lies just north of Crackington Haven (where refreshments and toilets are available) and is approached from Wainhouse Corner on A39. There are several car parking spaces on the road above the church (SX 149972).

Walk towards the cottages, then take the footpath to your left, signed COASTAL FOOTPATH. Through a kissing gate, then keep near the hedge on your right across a large field. Another gate takes you out onto the cliff, and to the coast path. Turn right.

Before long the path starts to descend, nearly to sea level, and then to climb the opposite side of the valley. At the top the path briefly follows a ridge with a drop to either side – not really dangerous, but some people may feel vertigo. After 600m you pass a gate, then a stile. Immediately after the stile turn sharp left, past a stile which has lost its fence, following the cliff edge.

At the next stile you need to take a decision. For the short circuit, don't cross it but turn right along the field hedge, and after 130 m you'll come to the fingerpost indicated as (*) in the text below.

For the full circuit, continue along the coast path. Cross a footbridge, then another stile, and continue over the next crest. When you reach a wire fence, don't cross the stile but turn right and follow the fence round two sides of the field, leaving the field at its top left by a gate. A metal gate ahead of you leads into a track which after 400 m brings you to Lower Tresmorn Farm.

Turn right through a gate (with white discs) and left along the field edge to another gate with

a high stile. Turn left along the track and you'll emerge on a gravelled area; ahead you'll see paddocks full of humps and bumps – which are actually the remains of a deserted medieval settlement.

Retrace your steps to the high stile and continue along the track, which abruptly turns left and down through a gate to Cleave Farm. Turn right (FOOTPATH) past 'The Barn', along a tarmac track and to the right of 'Abel's', and through a field gate to a fingerpost. (*)

Take the path signed CHURCH, downhill into sheltered woodland. Cross the stream and turn right. You will emerge in a largish field with a house on the far side. Head just to the left of the house and you will find a track which leads uphill back to the church car park. (Take the holloway, not the modern drive.)

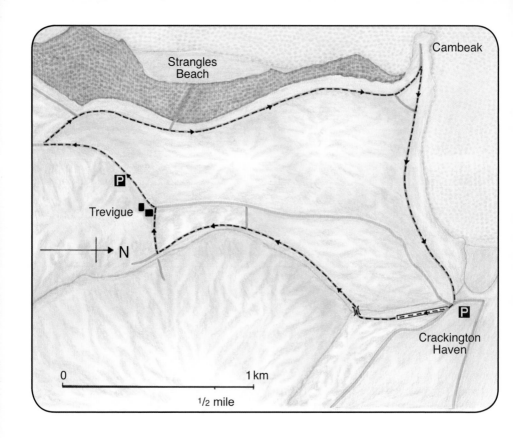

Walk 4   Crackington Haven

*Distance: 7.3km (4½ miles)   Time: 2 hours   OS Explorer sheet 111
Character: Attractive woodland, then spectacular coast. Numerous
butterfly species in Summer.*

Park at Crackington Haven (SX 143968), where there are cafés and
beach shops, toilets and a pub. There is an alternative starting point
just south of Trevigue (SX 135951), with free parking but no facilities.

Turn left out of the carpark. Go up the road past the turning to
Trevigue, then turn right opposite 'Coombe Cottages' along FOOTPATH
TO EAST WOOD. It starts as a private road, then after a gate becomes
a path. Cross a stream and after 30 m turn right towards SHEEPDIP.
Follow the path up the valley for 700 m: keep left (SHEEPDIP) and after
a further 650 m at a crossing of paths turn right (to TREVIGUE).

Climb up to Trevigue, where a gate just above the former farmhouse (now holiday lets in grounds lovingly manicured by the

National Trust) leads you out onto a lane. Turn left and after 600 m (having ignored a right turn through a kissing gate) turn right at a stile, signed TO THE COASTPATH. The footpath goes diagonally across a field, holding the contour, to another stile. Turn right along the coast path and continue for 1.5 km.

At a fork keep left (yellow arrow) and left again, up the side of Cambeak (though the first path on the right, with a white arrow, is a short cut if you need it). Follow the paths round the headland – where wild goats graze and the views are magnificent – then along the coast back into Crackington Haven.

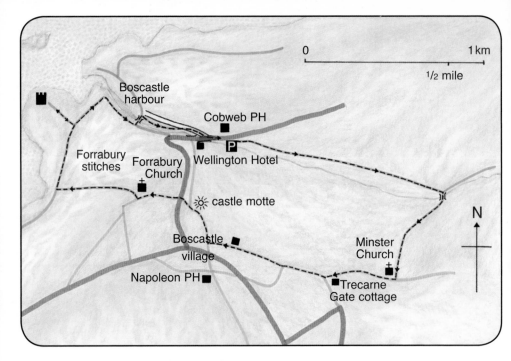

Map labels:
- Boscastle harbour
- Cobweb PH
- 0 — 1 km
- 1/2 mile
- Forrabury stitches
- Forrabury Church
- Wellington Hotel
- castle motte
- Boscastle village
- Minster Church
- N
- Napoleon PH
- Trecarne Gate cottage

Walk 5   Around Boscastle

Distance: 6 km (nearly 4 miles)   Time: Could be done in 1¹/₂ hours, if you ignored everything of interest on the way! Twice that is more likely. Character: A varied walk with woodland, cliff scenery and one of Cornwall's gems, the village and harbour of Boscastle, now largely recovered from the flood of August 2004. Two steep ascents.

If you want to understand more about what you are seeing, read Jim Castling's booklet What to see in Boscastle, *available in the village.*

Start from the main car park (SX 100912). Facilities include toilets, several shops, the Cobweb pub, cafés etc. Walk to the far end of the carpark where a path leads inland up the valley. After 1.3 km turn right across a footbridge (TO MINSTER CHURCH) and climb the path. Keep right at a fork; the path leads into the churchyard. Minster is the mother church of Boscastle, and it is thought there has been a religious foundation here for 1500 years.

Leave the churchyard by the path uphill, and turn right up the lane. At Trecarne Gate cottage, keep right. After nearly 300 m leave the lane by a stone stile on the right. Go through a field, over a stile, turn right over another stile and follow the wire fence on your left to a kissing gate. Don't cross the footbridge: continue down the path with the stream on your left.

Gander and Gunnera permitting, cross quietly in front of the house and walk up the driveway, which leads out onto the main street of the old village where you turn right. (You may want to make a short diversion for 200 m or so uphill to the second crossroads, above the 'Napoleon', to see some quaint old cottages.)

Descend High Street and, as it veers left, take a path on the right which soon leads to the Norman motte of Bottreaux Castle, which gave the village its name: not much to see, but a lovely outlook.

Continue down the old main street past the Post Office to a fork. Bear left, up to New Road. Turn left and immediately right up Forrabury Hill. Straight on up until,

opposite Sunny Bank, a path bears off to the right leading to the simple Norman church of St Symphorian. Notice the old cross outside the churchyard. Go through the churchyard, leaving by the gate at the top left corner; turn left down the track, past the Forrabury stitches – a remarkable survival of medieval strip farming, each strip still individually leased annually.

When you reach the coast path turn right. You will want to visit the white lookout tower, which has rather a good view.

Return to the gateway in the wall which defines the promontory, and turn left. Another time, you might like to try the path which bears off to the right, around the stitches, but this time descend all the way to the harbour. Cross the stream by the Witchcraft Museum and make your way inland to the main road, back to the carpark.

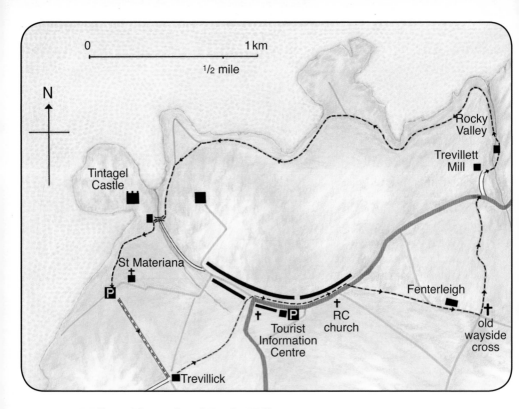

Walk 6   Tintagel and Rocky Valley

*Distance: 7.8 km (nearly 5 miles)   Time: 2¹/₂ hours – but it could be a
full day if you visit the castle and church. It can also be combined with
walk 7. OS Explorer sheet 111.*
*Character: One of my favourite walks, largely avoiding Tintagel village,
with superb scenery and generally less crowded than you might expect
so close to Tintagel. Very steep climbs.*

Start from the Tintagel Visitor Centre (SX 059883) which has explana-
tory displays; there are public toilets adjoining. From the car park
turn right along the main road. Pass the Catholic church and, 40 m
beyond Trenale Lane, turn right over a stile (PUBLIC FOOTPATH).

  Cross another stile at the end of the hedge on the left of the field.
From here the path heads towards a farmhouse called Fenterleigh,
three fields away, emerging on a lane – quite a busy one, so take care.

  Turn right, up to a crossroads (with an ancient waymark cross)
where you turn left (HALGABRON). Continue down this quiet lane,
ignoring tempting footpaths, then cross the B3263. The route is
signed TO THE COASTPATH; pass Trevillett Mill, cross the footbridge
and follow the path.

After 200 m you will reach the ruins of Trewethet Mill, which contain two maze carvings – possibly Bronze Age but more likely produced in Victorian times by a bored miller – which have become a shrine.

Turn left to cross the stream and follow the path down the far side. Keep left, joining the coast path and climbing steeply.

Follow the coast path west for more than 2 km (very steep in places) till you see Tintagel Haven with the Island and Castle ahead of you. Cross the stream and turn left past the English Heritage shop and exhibition, then immediately bear right up the footpath TO THE CHURCH.

Zig-zag up it, turning right at a junction and almost immediately left (unless you want to go into the castle – entry fee, but well worth it for the experience) and then keep right and right again.

Climb a stile, then head for Tintagel's isolated Norman church, St Materiana, which repays a proper visit. It contains a Roman milestone.

From the church go through the car park and follow a track parallel to the coast for 550 m till you come to a bungalow at a junction of tracks. Just before the bungalow, turn left over a stone stile along a footpath. Keep to the right of the telephone poles, then diagonally right to another stile, from which a path leads by way of five more stiles and a wooden bridge into the village. Emerging on the main street, turn right, back to the Visitor Centre.

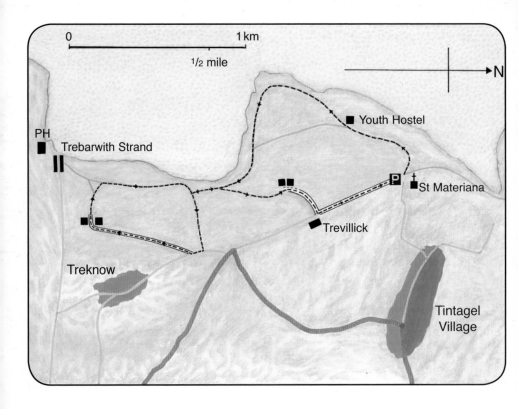

Walk 7   Tintagel and Trebarwith Strand

Distance: 5 km (3 miles) Time: 1 1/4 hours. It can be combined with walk 6 to make a full day's walk. OS Explorer sheet 111.
Character: Wonderful cliff scenery, with an inland return. A short and relatively level walk, the easiest in the book.

Park in the cliff carpark by St Materiana's church (SX 050884, National Trust, contributions requested). From the church end of the car park, walk along a cart-track (past a bicycle rack) towards the sea. This soon curves left. At a complex junction of paths, bear right downhill, in the direction of a conical island.

Pass above the Youth Hostel and leave the track by a path to the right, noticing evidence of former slate quarrying, including platforms constructed to hold derricks. Round the headland. At a wooden stile turn right and after 50 m cross a stone stile onto Bagalow cliffs.

Before long you will pass the head of a deep gulley, where a wire fence is supported by rectangular slabs of slate. 10 m beyond this turn left at a stile (notable for a piece of white 'marble' built into it) with a path across a field. Cross this field and the next, then turn right along

16

An abandoned slate quarry on the cliffs just north of Trebarwith Strand, with a grotesque stack of poor quality rock left as a sentinel

a lane for 150 m. When the lane bears left, carry straight on along a private road for 500 m. The road or track ends at a group of houses, but a footpath continues downhill towards Trebarwith Strand, a popular cove and beach, with shops, a café, and a pub which has excellent views from its terrace: you may well want to make a diversion at this point!

If not, then at the first junction of paths bear right, then wind uphill to a T-junction of paths. Turn right, and follow the coast path for 1 km past some extraordinary pillars of rock: the slate here was presumably of inferior quality and so rejected.

When you arrive back at the stile with the white 'marble', continue for just 20 m. Where the coast path turns left along the cliff edge, keep straight on, beside the wall. Cross two fields, then follow a track straight ahead past the white houses.

At Trevillick Farm crossroads, turn left (TO THE COASTPATH) along a track which leads back to the church and your car.

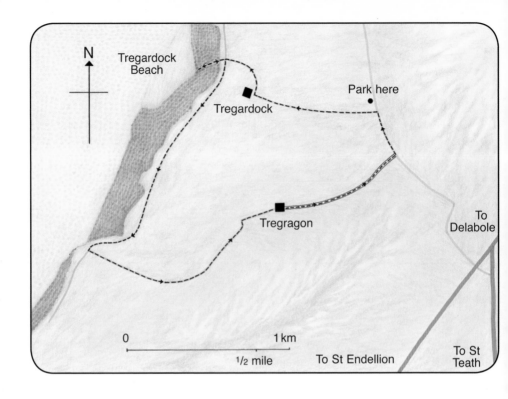

Walk 8   Tregardock Beach

Distance: 6.3 km (4 miles)   Time: 2 hours   OS Explorer sheet 111
Character: Superb cliffs (care needed with children and dogs),
a wonderful expanse of beach and a pleasant inland return. Several
steep ascents and descents.

Parking: one mile south from Delabole, turn right to TRELIGGA. After
1 km, just beyond the left turn to Tregardock, there is parking for 4
cars (SX 053838). For this walk, there is no point in parking down the
lane to Tregardock, which becomes very congested in summer with
people going to the beach. You will not shorten the walk that way!

   Walk down the lane signed to Tregardock Farm. Just before the
farm entrance, turn right through a gate, TO THE COASTPATH. After
120 m go through a kissing gate, and then after 50 m keep left. Shortly,
a gate leads you onto Tregardock Cliffs (National Trust).

   When you reach a crossroads of paths, carry straight on to Tregardock Beach, which even at high tide is well worth a visit for its scenic
qualities. When exposed there is plenty of room for everyone: the long
walk back to the car tends to deter families with young children.

Tregardock Beach

Return uphill 300 m to the 'crossroads' and turn right along the coastpath until you come to a little footbridge. Ignore the stile on your left (unless you need a short cut) and begin a major descent. At the bottom, before the stream, turn left across a stile, heading up a wild and deserted valley.*

After two gates, a well defined path leads steadily uphill: it's quite a long drag! At the top turn left over a stile and immediately right over another one. Head for the farm. Over a stile, then between the farm buildings; follow a concrete road gently uphill till you reach a tarmac lane. Turn left, and in 300 m you will reach your car.

* You could now choose to extend your walk south along the coastpath for as long as you like, returning later to this point. To help you decide: from here back to your car is 2.5 km (1¹/₂ miles), including a longish ascent, taking perhaps 45 minutes.

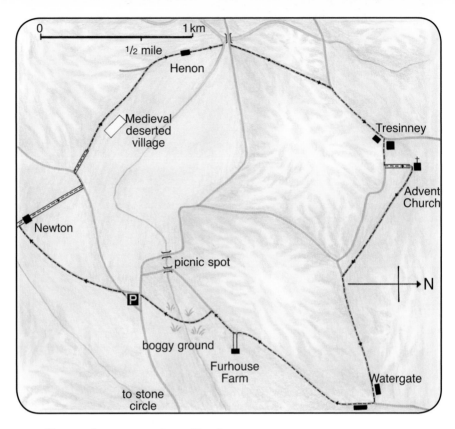

Walk 9   Advent, near Camelford

*Distance: 8.5 km (5¹/₄ miles)   Time: 2¹/₂ hours   OS Explorer sheet 109
Character: Moorland edge, where farming is a tough business. Includes
a deserted medieval village, and an unspoiled old church where some of
the congregation are bats – of the rare Brown long-eared variety.
No significant hills, but innumerable stiles. The nettles become tall and
vigorous so don't go bare-legged.*

Start at Harpur's Downs. To get there from Camelford, take the lane
from Tregoodwell (at the north end of the town) towards Roughtor,
and turn right at a crossroads, signed ADVENT CHURCH.

At two junctions keep left then follow a narrow lane till you cross
a stream – a picnic spot. At a T-junction turn left. After 300 m, there
is a triangle of grass at a road junction. Park here (SX 115798). When
you've done the walk, don't miss the stone circle at SX 126800; drive
towards, then past the Stannon china clay works; the circle lies on the
right just beyond where the tarmac gives out.

Start by following a path south-west, away from the china clay pits.

It is indicated by a yellow arrow on a wooden post. (After very wet weather, you may want to stick to the lane. See map.) Cross 5 stiles, then pass through a wood and emerge onto an old track. Turn right up it, past a farm (Newton) and on up to a lane.

Turn left, and after 80m, when the lane bends, take the track straight on through a gate and through a yard, then up a holloway (a medieval track) which leads to and through the deserted village of Carwether. At the top of the slope its ruins are clearly visible as humps and bumps to the right of the track. The village has gone but its right of way remains! Notice where it broadens at the village centre.

Follow the holloway down, keeping to the left when it gets over-grown, and through a metal gate. At a barn, keep right and pass through Henon to cross a stream by a clapper bridge. Cross the lane and take the PUBLIC FOOTPATH opposite, through a gate. Keep the hedge to your right across two fields, then straight across the third, which brings you to a lane: turn right up the lane to Tresinney village. At the road junction turn right and after 100m turn left, signed ADVENT CHURCH. Turn right into the churchyard.

Leave the churchyard by a stile at the far (east) end – continue straight across the field, don't turn right. Follow waymarked stiles over 5 fields. Leave by a stile (not the gate) and turn left along the lane. After 1km at a junction turn right, then after a further 1.2km (200m beyond the entrance to Furhouse Farm) turn left across a stile (PUBLIC FOOTPATH). Head through the glade (the ruins of a settlement) and descend the slope. Cross a boggy area by stepping stones then follow the waymarked path, which will bring you to your car.

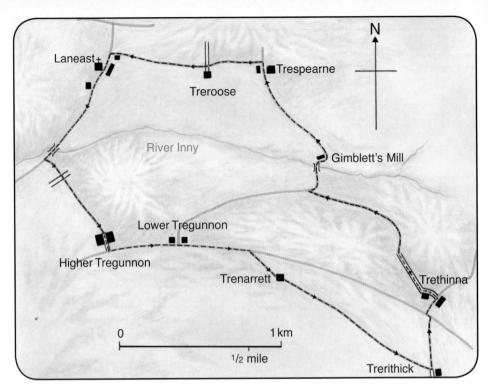

Walk 10   An inland walk, from Laneast

Distance: 7.3 km (4¹/₂ miles) Time: 2 hours OS Explorer Sheet 109
Character: Very rural, giving a delightful taste of inland North
Cornwall, where agriculture struggles to survive and tourism is seen
only in the form of genteel holiday lets and 'second homes'.
One stiffish ascent, but 22 stiles, not all of them user-friendly.

Laneast is a village lying south of A 395, and due north of Altarnun.
Start at the church (SX 228840). From the church gate, turn right
(downhill) along the lane to a bridge. After another 50 m turn left over
a waymarked stile; after 15 m bear right uphill through a wood. After
a steepish climb, cross the track and stiles into a field and continue in
the same direction to a waymarked stile (40 m left of a metal gate).

Through the next field, keeping to the right; through gate, turning
right on a farm track, which then turns left between farm buildings.
Turn left into a quiet lane and continue past a crossroads for 850 m,
where a footpath on the right is signed to OLDHAY. Diagonally left
across the field, through a gateway and then to the right of poly-
tunnels, to a wooden gate and stile at the bottom of the field. Through
a metal gate and turn left along the track, passing 2 cottages then
turning right before the third, and through a 7-bar gate.

Proceed down the track, then through waymarked gates, keeping to the top of fields. In time you'll find yourself crossing a stile on the edge of a field. Facing out, at 'one o'clock' there is a tall wooden stile: head for that and then another beyond. Keep beside a hedge on your right across the next field; cross a stile, and head for the gates hidden at the far left corner of the field. Take the gate which leads down a track, to Trerithick Farm. Just before the farm, turn left through a gate. Keep the row of tall trees on your left. A stile at the far left corner of the field leads to a lane. Turn left and in 20 m right, then in 100 m left, signed PUBLIC FOOTPATH.

Follow this path through two gates; after a third gate turn right and do a dog-leg along two sides of the field. Over a stile, across the next field (45° right) to a stile. Then to a gateway mid-way up the opposite hedge. Follow a delightful path to a lane, where you turn right passing Gimblett's Mill, and up the lane to a farm. 30 m beyond 'Trespearne Barn', turn left through an unmarked gate into a little used track.

A waymarked stile leads into a field; aim just to the left of the large barn, cross the stile, turn left and in 20 m turn right over a stile. Down the left side of the field and across the stream and stile. The footpath cuts across the corner of a field to another stile, and over a second stream.

Bear right uphill, to the left of a row of houses ahead, and through a gate. There's a stile by the barn in the far left corner of the field. Follow signs through the farmyard and back down to the church.

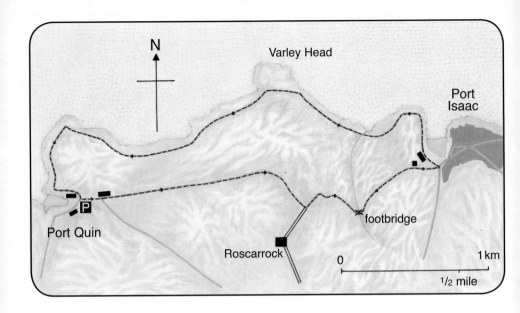

Walk 11   Port Quin to Port Isaac

Distance: 8 km (5 miles)   Time: 2¼ hours plus time at Port Isaac
OS Explorer 106

*Character: Initially quiet rural, then a delightful view of Port Isaac,
then a magnificent coastal section. Very steep ascents and descents,
many steps. Quite a demanding walk.*

Park in the National Trust carpark at Port Quin (donations requested – and well deserved for the work they do along this coast) at
SS 972805.

Leave the carpark by the vehicle entrance, turn right and walk up
the lane for 150 m. Bear left across the front of the cottages (PUBLIC
FOOTPATH PORT ISAAC 2). From a stile, this is an easily followed path
then track through a landscape of broad rolling fields.

Pass through 3 gateways (with stiles, but the gates are often open).
At the fourth gateway, some 200 m before you reach Roscarrock farm,
the track turns sharp right, but you instead go through the gateway
and turn sharp left towards the sea, alongside the hedge and round the
field border to a stile.

Descend into the valley bottom to a footbridge. Take the path uphill
on the far side: emerging from the bushes, head straight up to and
past an old lookout post: there's a stile one third of the way up the
far hedge.

From the next field there are wonderful views of Port Isaac – but don't go too far!

Your path lies just beside the left hedge, and becomes a holloway – an old track worn down by centuries of horse traffic so that it becomes a watercourse in winter, and muddy even in summer. It brings you to the edge of Port Isaac. You need to turn left onto the coastal path – but it would be surprising if you didn't want to explore Port Isaac first.

The return along the coast path requires no directions: just proceed for 5 km. It is quite tough going but the scenery will sustain you!

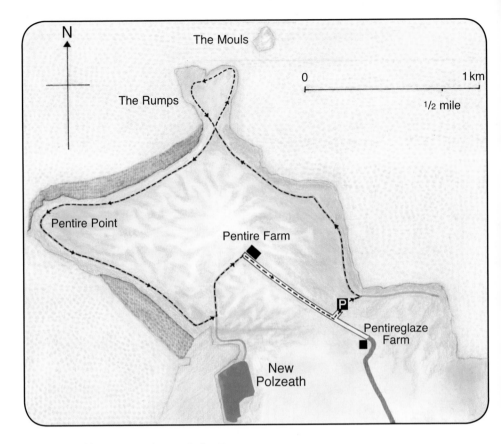

Walk 12 Pentire and the Rumps

Distance: 6.5 km (4 miles) Time: 2 hours OS Explorer Sheet 106
Character: Superb cliff scenery, and only a short inland stretch.

Park at the National Trust carpark just beyond Pentireglaze (SW 941800). To get there, take the POLZEATH/NEW POLZEATH turning off the B 3314, pass the Bee Centre and bear right.

Then take the second turning on the right (at a crossroads) and drive through Pentireglaze farm, and take the first carpark offered on the right. This is in fact on the site of a former lead mine.

Leave by the path past the contributions box up over some spoil heaps and across a small field. Go through the gate and turn left along the coast path. On a clear day you can see as far as Hartland Point, over 50 km (30 miles) away. After 500 m you will see ahead of you 'the Rumps': the name derives from the Anglo-Saxon and is not Cornish! It is a distinctive double headland which was fortified in the Iron Age. Cross the outer ditch and rampart at a gateway.

Explore the area whichever way you like, but a walk around the right buttock gives perhaps the most interesting views, of rock formations and an island called The Mouls. However, the view from the top of the left buttock is more extensive. Return to the gateway and turn right, which will lead you to Pentire Point and on to Pentire Haven, where the path skirts a deep sandy inlet.

From the head of the cove a path leads inland up the valley. On reaching slate-hung Pentire Farm, turn right up the track which will lead you back to your car.

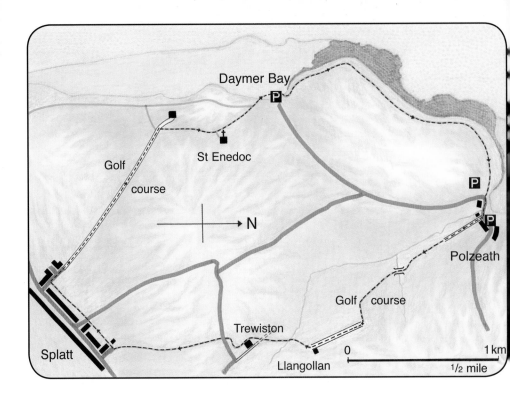

Walk 13   Polzeath and Daymer Bay

*Distance: 8.7 km (5¹/₂ miles)   Time: 2 hours.   OS Explorer sheet 106
Character: A pleasant easy walk if you're staying in Polzeath or Rock,
consisting of farmland, golf courses, estuary and seashore. Beaches and
rockpools for the young at heart. Take care within the golf courses!*

From the beach at Polzeath (SW 937789) take the PUBLIC BYWAY
between the Post Office and Stotts the newsagents. Pass between a
caravan park and a row of elevated bungalows, and up a track. Cross
a stream, then after 200 m a stile, entering a golf course, climbing and
keeping an old hedgebank on your right.

Continue in the same direction across the fairways; when you reach
the hedge keep left along it for 330 m then turn right up a waymarked
track, to the centre of this golf course complex, once Llangollan farm.
Take the footpath ahead signed TREWISTON, bearing slightly right, to
find a stile in a tall hedge.

Leaving the golf course the path cuts diagonally across the corner
of a field to a stile, then across the next field in the same direction. If
there are crops and the path has not been re-established, go round the

28

edge of the field to the right, to a stone stile; cross a farm track and go round Trewiston Farm, outside a barbed wire fence. Follow the field edge to a stone stile. Cross a narrow field in the same direction, turn right at the hedge and in 30 m turn left at a stile. Cross to the far right corner of the field, where a stile leads into a lane. Cross the lane.

The footpath continues across four more fields (the exit from the second is at 'one o'clock' but if the path has not been re-established you may need to go along two sides of the field, keeping the hedge on your left) and out onto a track between houses in the village of Splatt.

After 50 m of the track, turn right (waymarked) past Manor Cottage and to the left of Maidenover along a back alley. Cross a road – Trewint Lane – and continue up the lane opposite, which soon becomes a track. At a crossroads, turn right past a few bungalows and out along a tarmac track which leads to and through a rather picturesque golf links, which I am told is in the top 100 UK courses: it certainly looks testing. Some 150 m short of a glade of trees, bear right off the track (waymarked) across a bridge. Turn left, which brings you to St Enedoc church. (Walk to the left of the fairway and the green, not on them!) The path now becomes a track. When it forks, bear left and follow the white stone markers till you reach the beach: turn right along it.

Go up the steps and turn left across the front of the carpark, where the facilities include a shop and toilets, and follow the coast path (nearly flat, wide and rather well populated) for 2 km back to Polzeath.

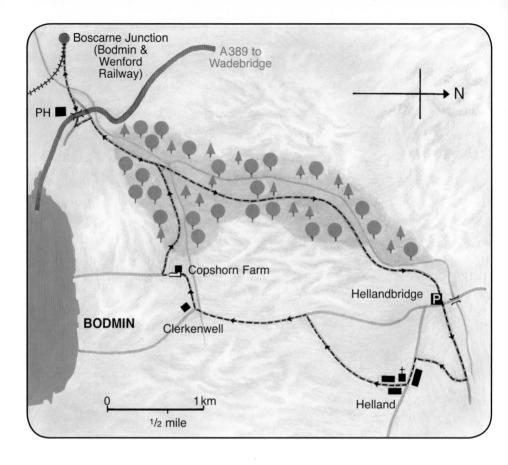

Walk 14   Hellandbridge to Dunmere

*Distance: 10.5 km (6 1/2 miles) Time: 2 1/4 hours OS Explorer sheet 109
The extension to Boscarne Junction and back adds 4 km (2 1/2 miles)
and takes an extra hour. This walk can alternatively be done from
Boscarne Junction, reached by preserved steam railway from Bodmin.*

*Character: Different from the other walks in this book: a little longer
– much longer if you include Boscarne – but very easy walking –
relatively flat, almost entirely on hard surfaces (tracks and some very
quiet lanes) with few stiles. An attractive inland walk through pleasant
farming country, then wonderful mixed woodland.*

Park at Hellandbridge (SX 065714). From the carpark, which was a
wharf on the old railway line, cross the lane and proceed east along
the Camel Trail for 1 km. At some farm buildings, turn right up a
lane passing through the hamlet of Bodwen. At a T-junction turn left.
After 300 m turn right at the war memorial, go through the attractive

hamlet of Helland, and continue for 1.2 km until you reach a T-junction, where you turn left. After 1 km, at the bottom of a hill and just before a roadside cottage ('Old Laundry') turn right along an unsigned track.

Keep left at a fork after 400 m. Climb to and past Copshorn farm: the track becomes tarmac. At the top of the slope turn right through a gate along a gravel track which, after several gates, leads into woodland.

Head down towards the valley bottom, keeping left when a more used forestry track sweeps off to the right.

You will soon reach a cross-track which runs parallel to the Camel Trail. At this point you can turn right and join

the Trail in 100 m or so, and it will take you back to Hellandbridge.

However, you can make an interesting extension by keeping left, and joining the Trail after a further 500 m. You will reach a sign which tells cyclists and walkers to turn left. To go straight on here is possible, and saves perhaps 300 m, but it brings you to a seriously dangerous road crossing. Play safe and follow the track to the left for 350 m, then double back right along the disused railway line.

This was the Bodmin & Wadebridge, one of the earliest steam railways in the world, opened in 1834. If you proceed past the defunct platform of Dunmere Junction (with useful access to the Borough Arms pub) for another 600 m you will reach Boscarne Junction, served by the steam trains of the Bodmin & Wenford Railway.

The return to Hellandbridge is simplicity itself: just follow the Camel Trail for 6 km through some lovely woodland.

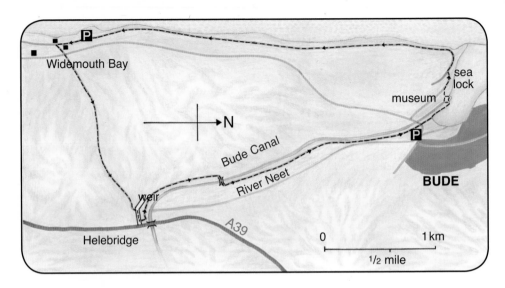

Walk 15 Widemouth & Bude

*Distance: 9.2 km (5 3/4 miles)   Time: 2 1/4 hours   OS Explorer sheet 111
Character: Easy walking, pleasant farmland, then the Bude Canal which
is quite unlike any other Cornish landscape, then low clifftops.*

You could start this walk from the carpark by the Bude Visitor Centre,
but I prefer to park in the (currently free) carpark just north of
Widemouth Bay Post Office (SS 199032). This saves the cliff scenery
for the end of the walk.

From the telescope and information point, take the path south,
towards the beach and parallel to the road. Pass seaward of one house,
then at the second house turn left, up to the road. Cross 'Marine Drive'
and take the PUBLIC FOOTPATH opposite, which is a well-beaten path.

After 1.8 km this emerges on a track. Turn right, and before crossing
the Bude Canal turn left – there is no need to go onto the main road.
Join the towpath and follow it for 2.5 km, crossing the canal mid-way,
till you reach a carpark (toilets and Visitor Centre). Cross the busy
road at the road bridge and continue down the right bank, past the
Bude-Stratton Museum.

Cross the canal at the sea-lock, turn right, climb steps to a road and
continue to more steps, at the top of which you turn right onto the
COASTPATH. Follow this for 3km back to Widemouth Bay.